Catherine Rollin

COMPLETE COLLECTION

T0103168

Lyric Moments

22 Expressive Solos for Intermediate to Early Advanced Pianists

"These lyric moments reflect spontaneous expressions of very special feelings and experiences. It is my hope that these pieces will evoke heartfelt emotions in those who perform and hear them."

Catherine Rollin

All 22 of the expressive solos in the three books of the *Lyric Moments* series are included in this complete edition. Book 1 (pages 2–20) is dedicated to Catherine's daughter, Summer. Book 2 (pages 21–41) is dedicated to the memory of Catherine's friend and mentor, the composer William Gillock. Book 3 (pages 42–64) has multiple dedications to friends, colleagues, and family. These pieces aim to inspire those who perform them to express their innermost feelings and to convey those feelings to their audiences.

Alfred Music
P.O. Box 10003
Van Nuys, CA 91410-0003
alfred.com

Copyright © 2015 by Alfred Music
All rights reserved.   Produced in USA.

No part of this book shall be reproduced, arranged, adapted, recorded, publicly performed, stored in a retrieval system, or transmitted by any means without written permission from the publisher. In order to comply with copyright laws, please apply for such written permission and/or license by contacting the publisher at alfred.com/permissions.

ISBN-10: 1-4706-2616-0
ISBN-13: 978-1-4706-2616-7
Cover art: *Sunset at Sea* (1911)
By Childe Hassam (1859-1935), Oil on canvas

A Special Place in My Heart

Catherine Rollin

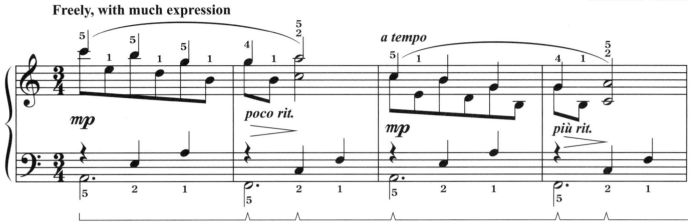

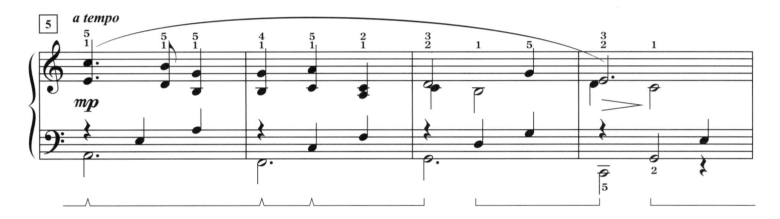

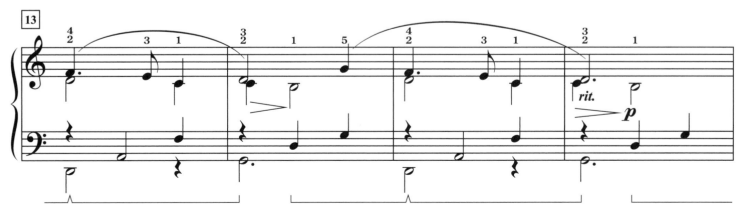

Copyright © 1995 by Alfred Music
All rights reserved..

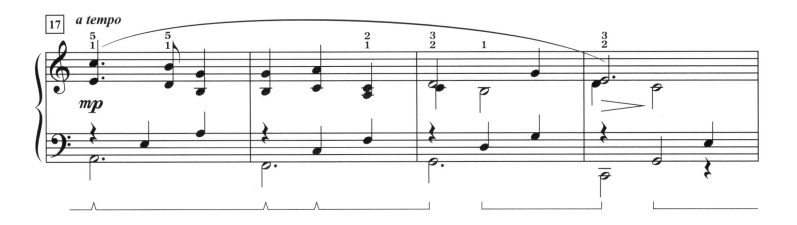

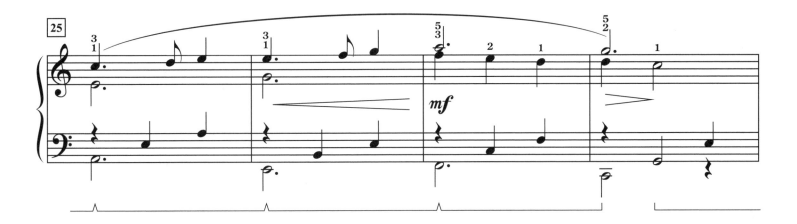

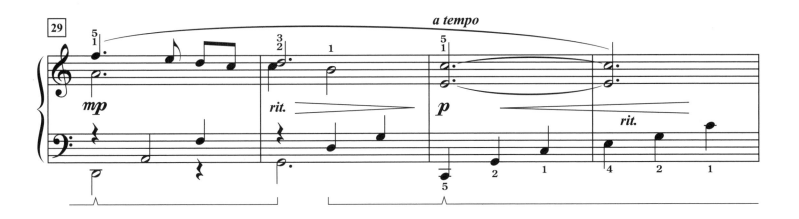

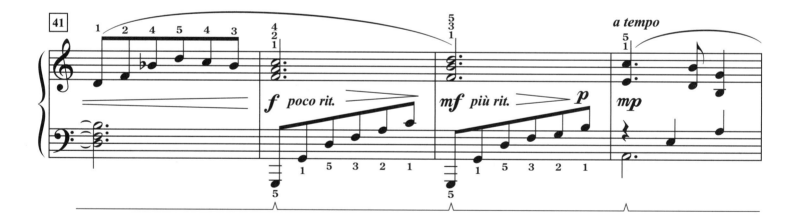

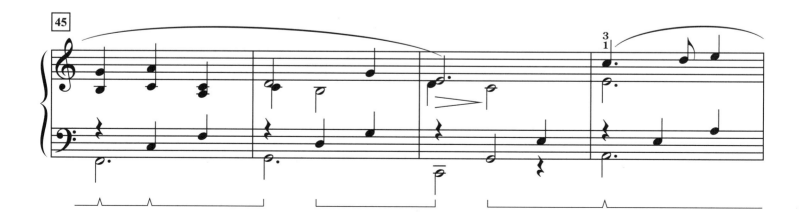

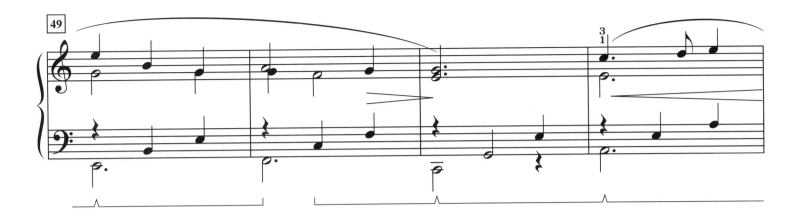

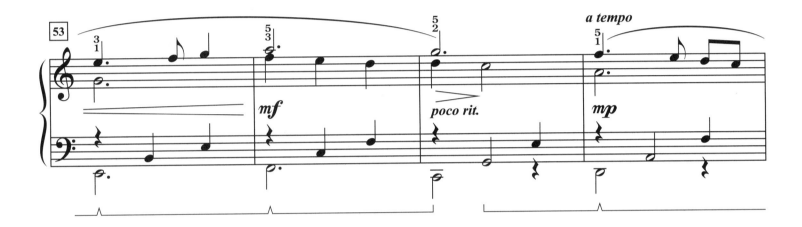

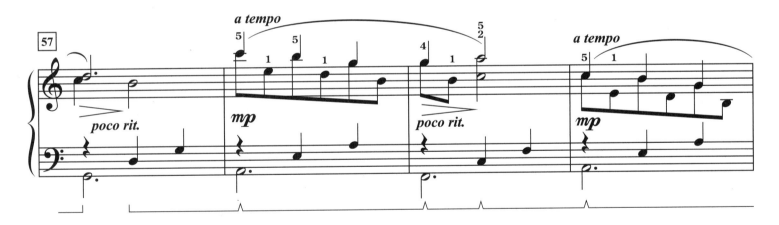

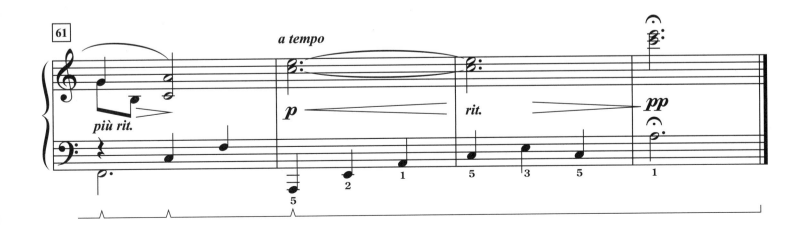

Sweet Memories

Catherine Rollin

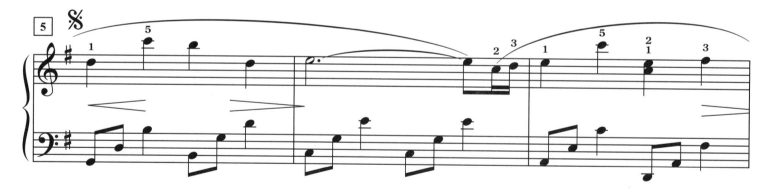

Copyright © 1995 by Alfred Music
All rights reserved..

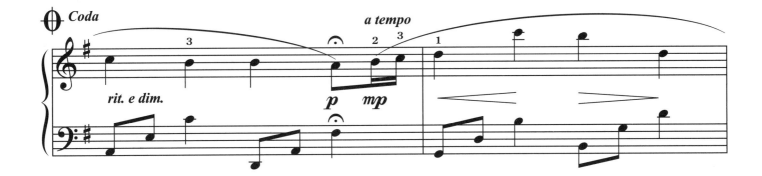

Summer's Dream

Catherine Rollin

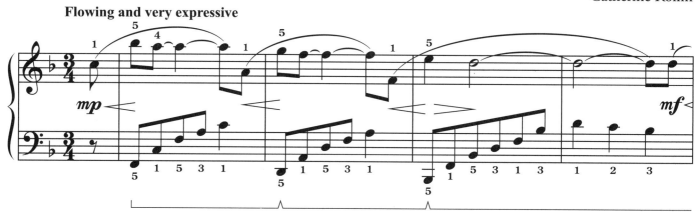

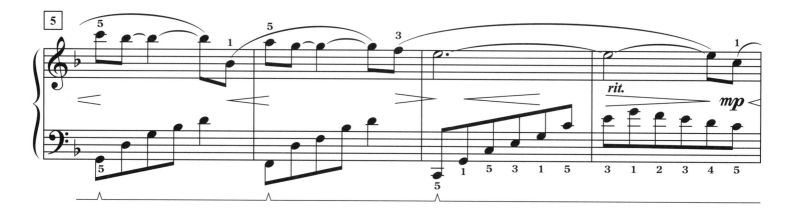

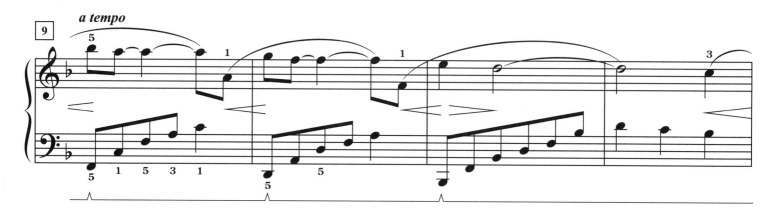

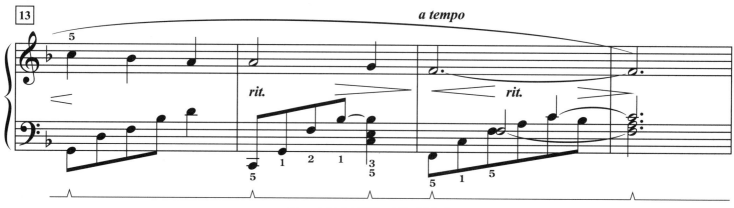

Copyright © 1995 by Alfred Music
All rights reserved..

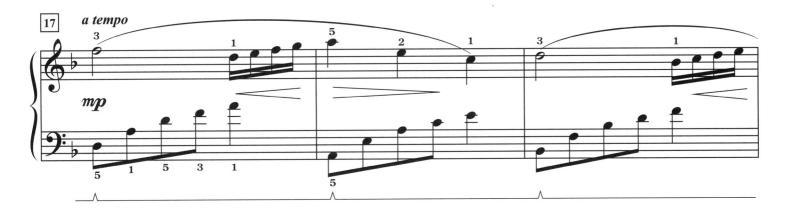

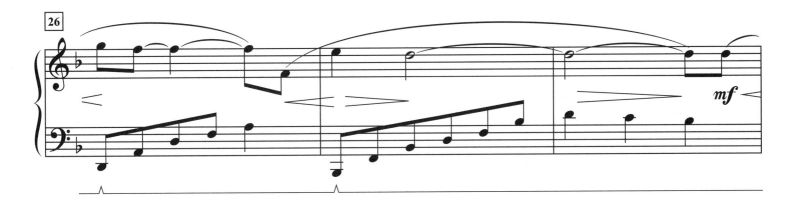

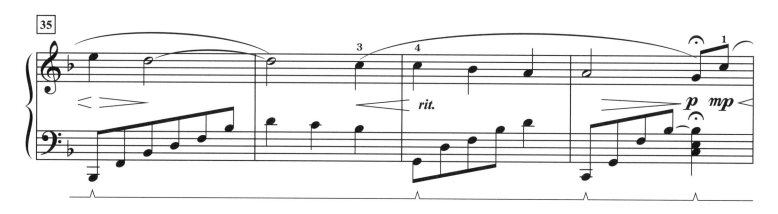

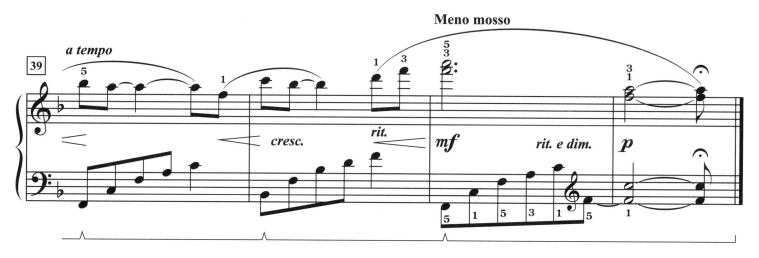

Tender Moments

Catherine Rollin

Copyright © 1995 by Alfred Music
All rights reserved..

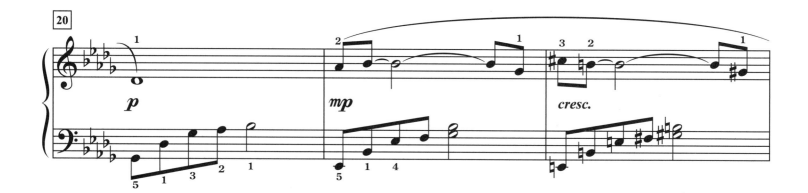

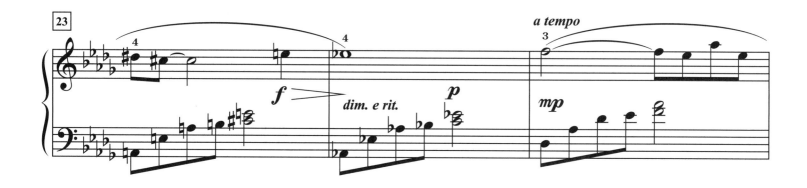

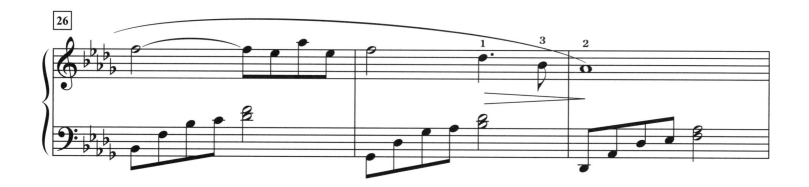

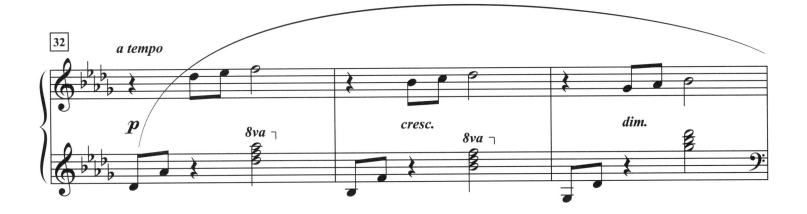

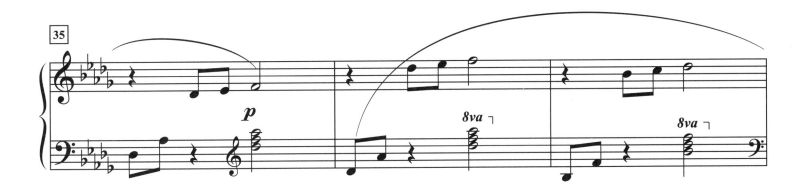

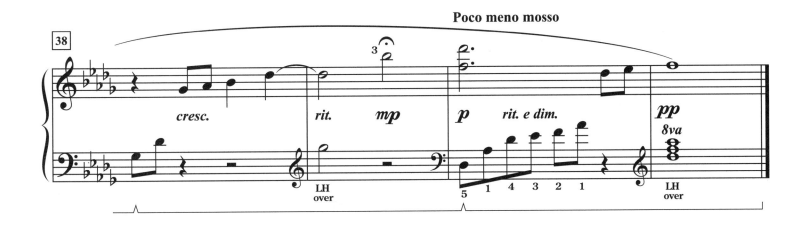

A Song for You

Catherine Rollin

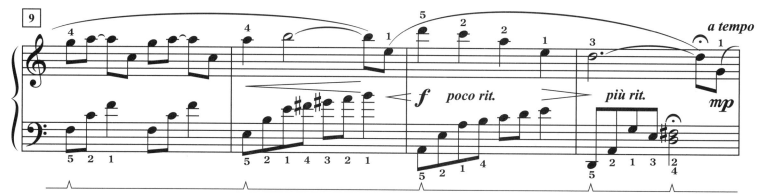

Copyright © 1995 by Alfred Music
All rights reserved..

Summer's Nocturne

Catherine Rollin

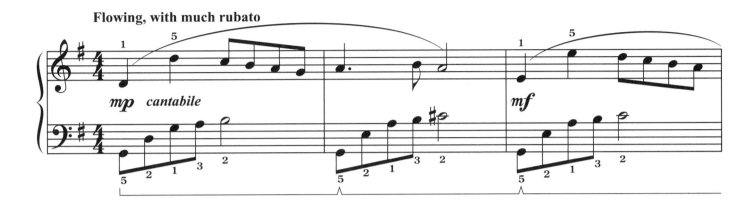

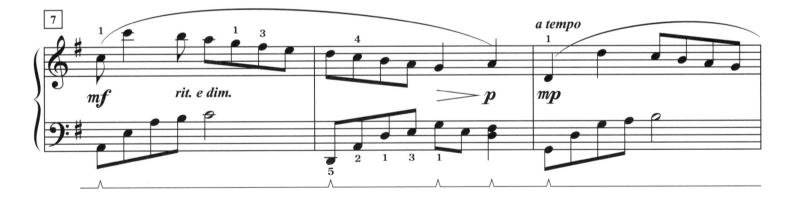

Copyright © 1995 by Alfred Music
All rights reserved..

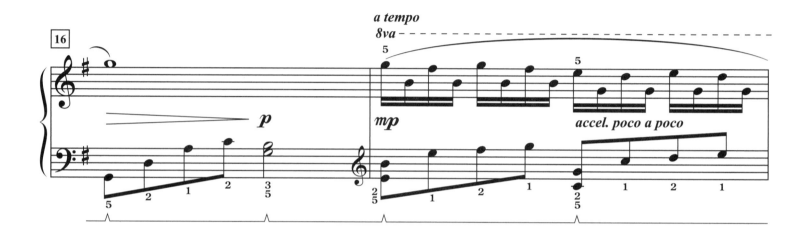

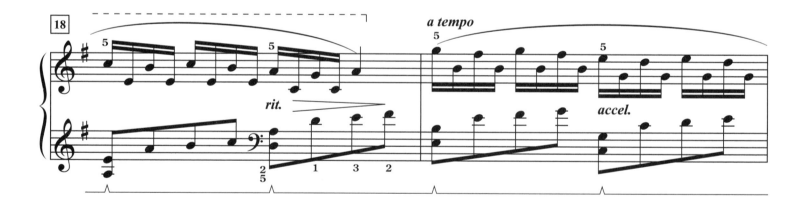

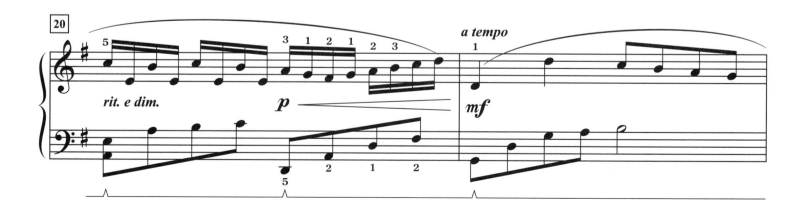

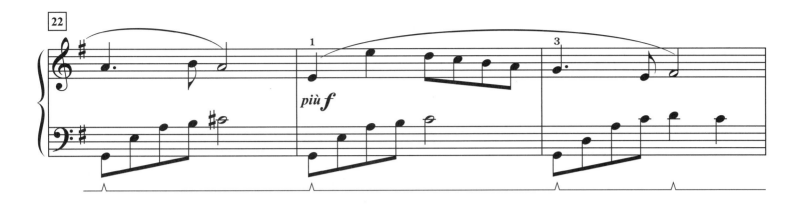

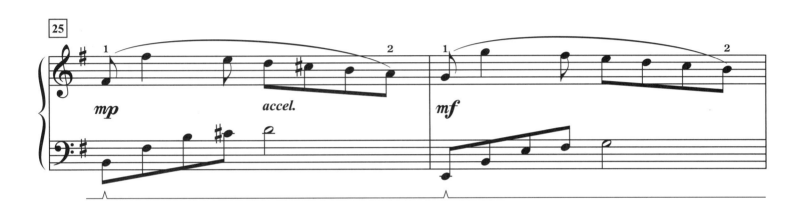

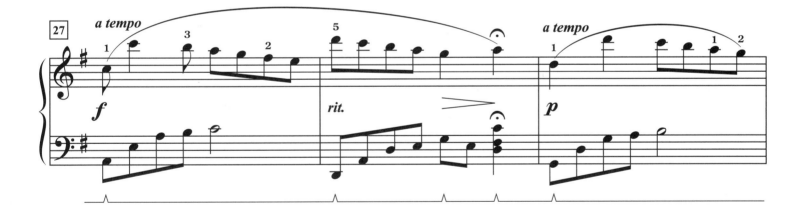

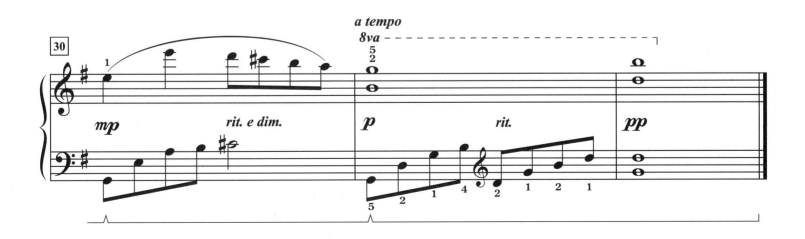

Lullaby and Dreamland

Catherine Rollin

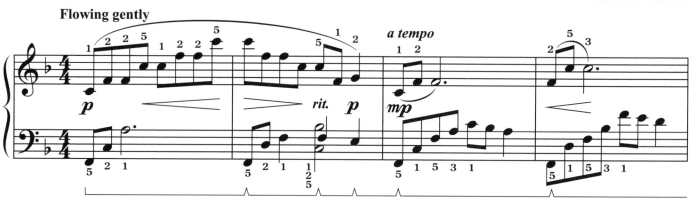

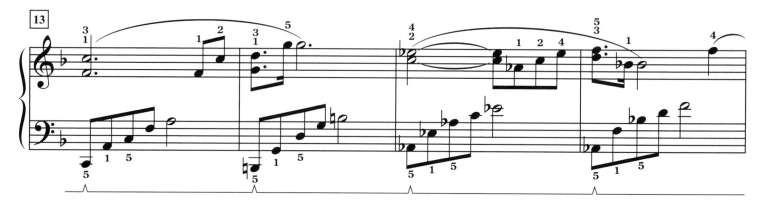

Copyright © 1995 by Alfred Music
All rights reserved..

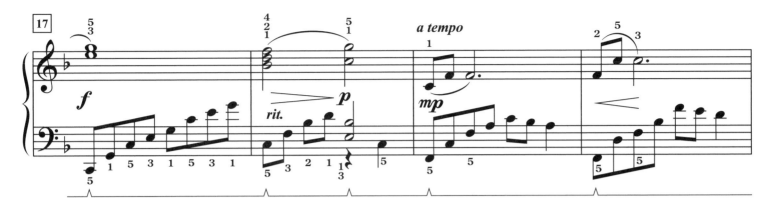

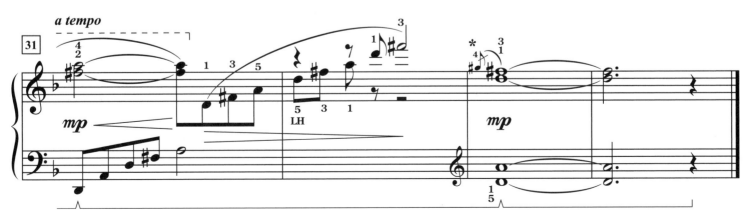

* The grace note should be played before the beat.

Thinking of Summer

Moderately, with much lyricism

Catherine Rollin

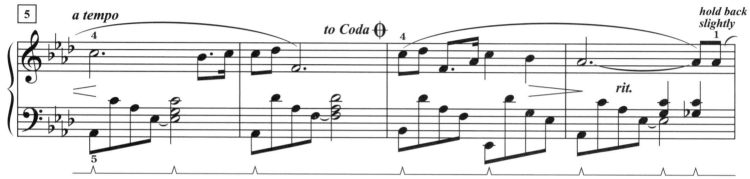

Copyright © 1995 by Alfred Music
All rights reserved..

A Heart Takes Flight

Catherine Rollin

Singing and with solid rhythm

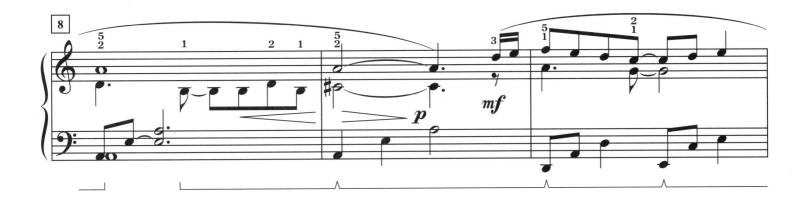

Copyright © 1995 by Alfred Music
All rights reserved..

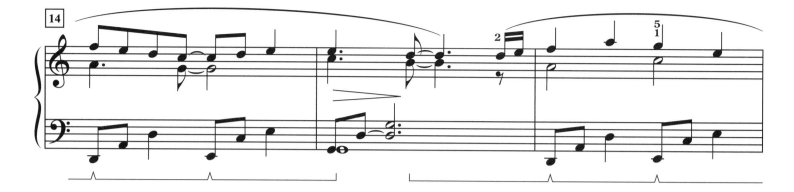

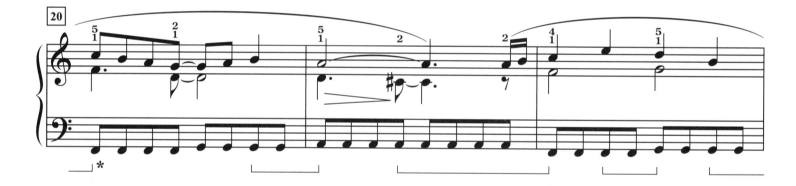

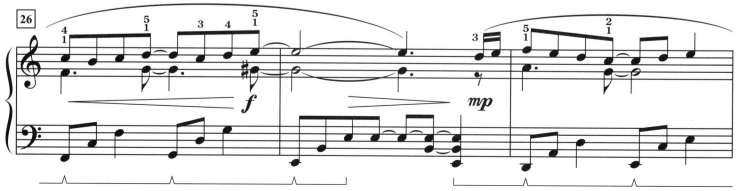

* In measures 20–25, the LH should be detached and the pedal should be used sparingly,
  so as not to change the character of the LH.

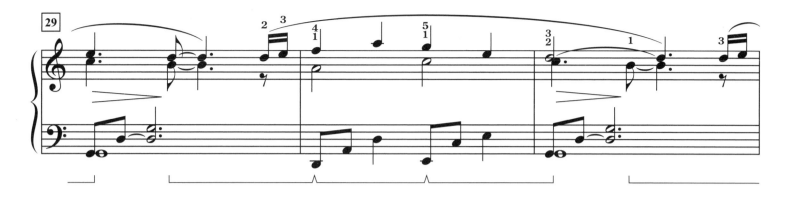

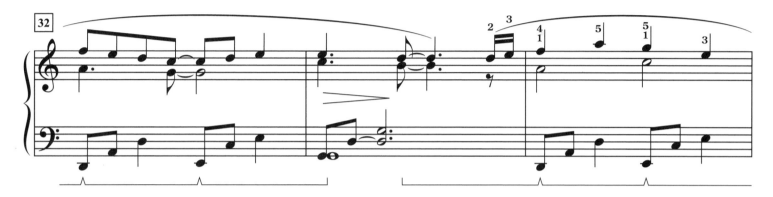

Daydream

Catherine Rollin

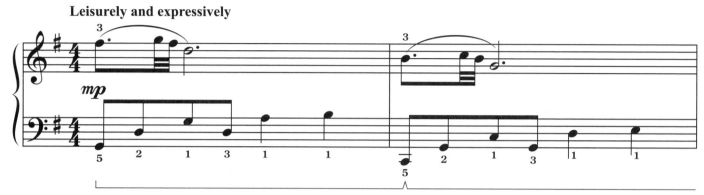

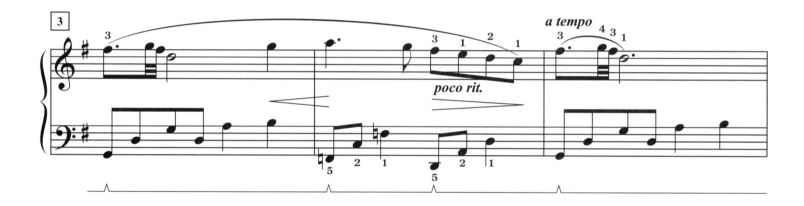

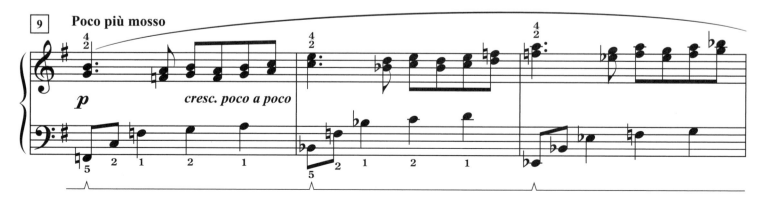

Copyright © 1995 by Alfred Music
All rights reserved..

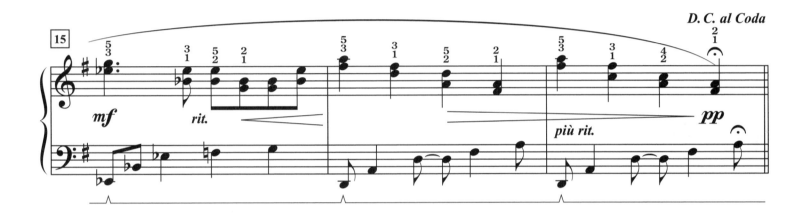

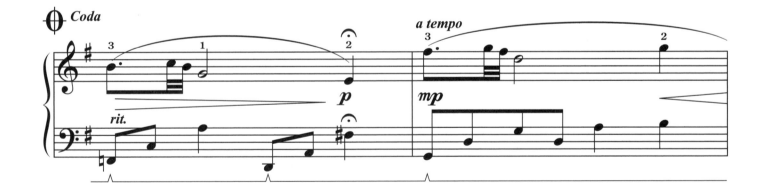

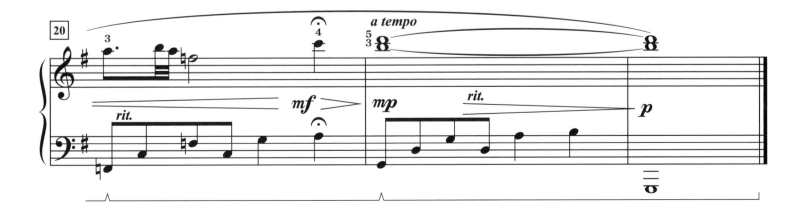

Simple Pleasures

Catherine Rollin

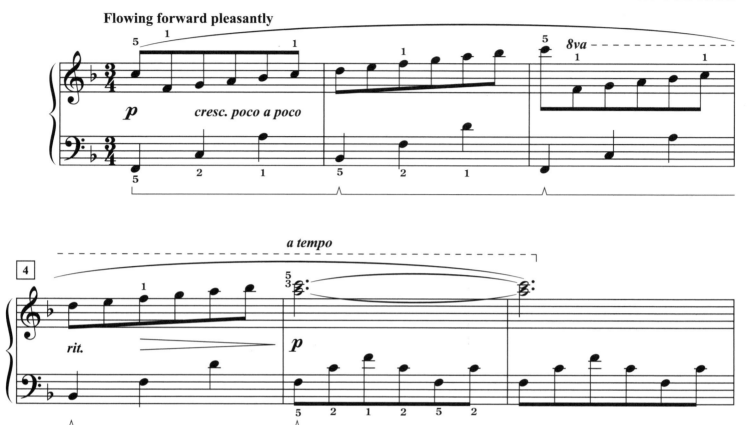

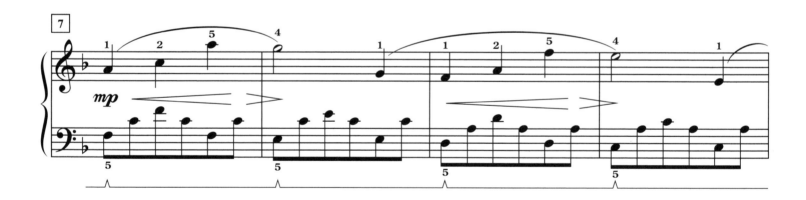

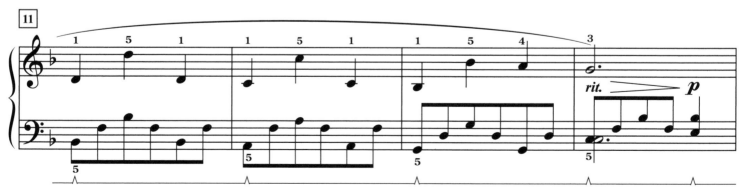

Copyright © 1995 by Alfred Music
All rights reserved..

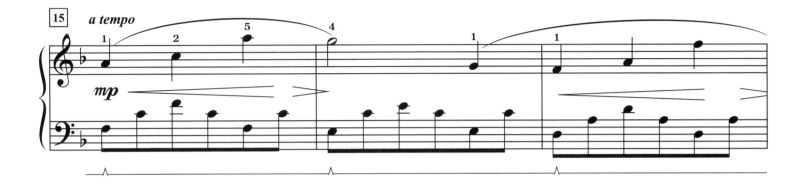

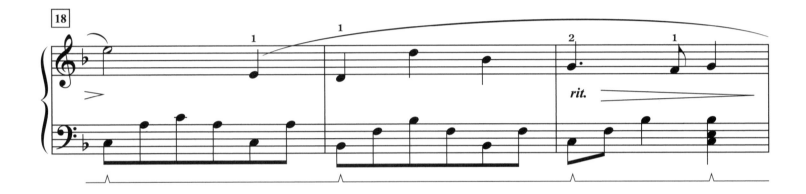

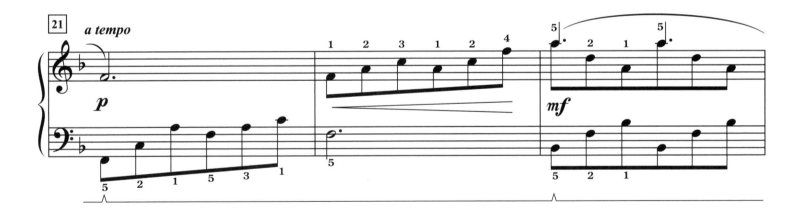

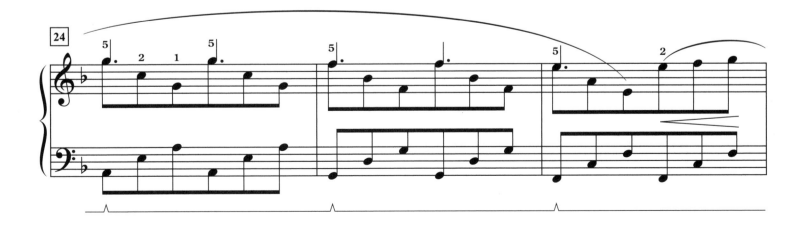

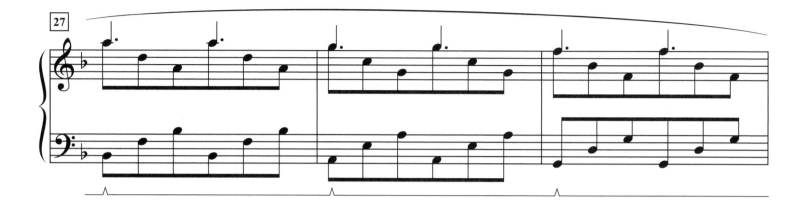

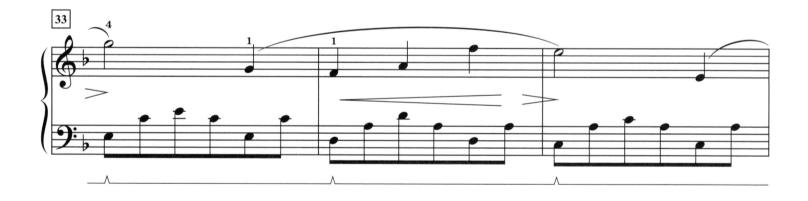

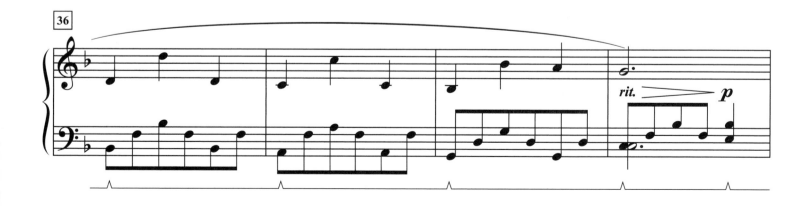

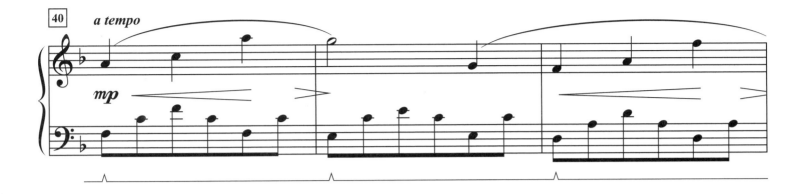

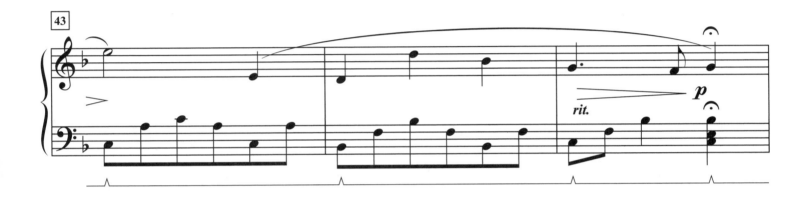

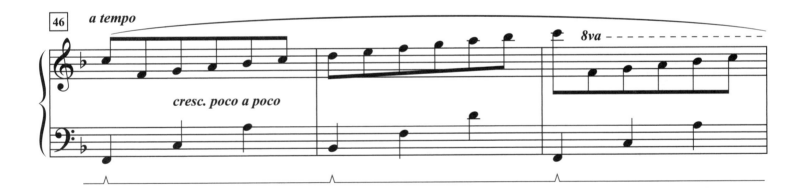

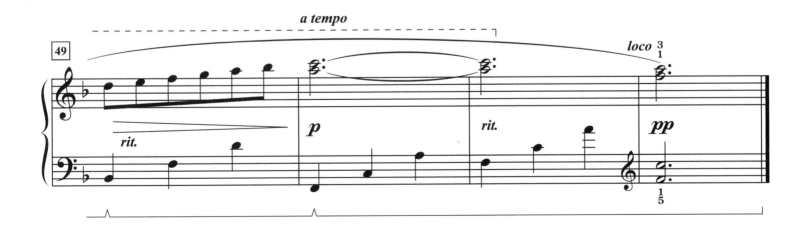

Love Theme

Catherine Rollin

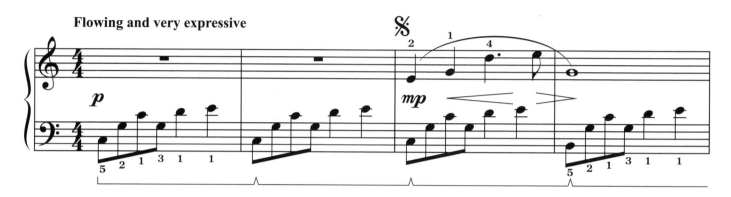

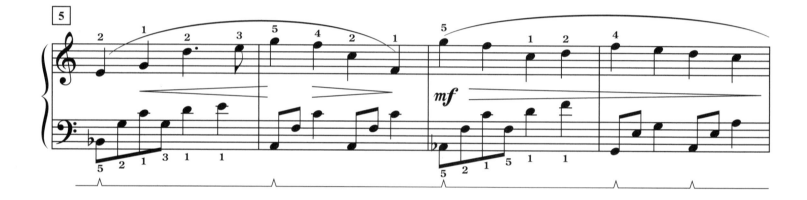

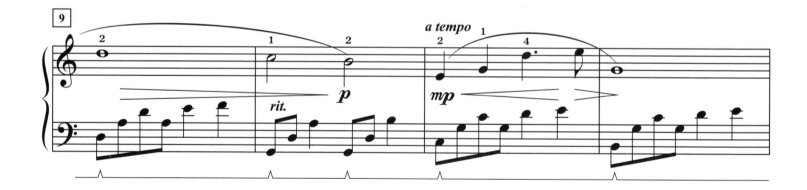

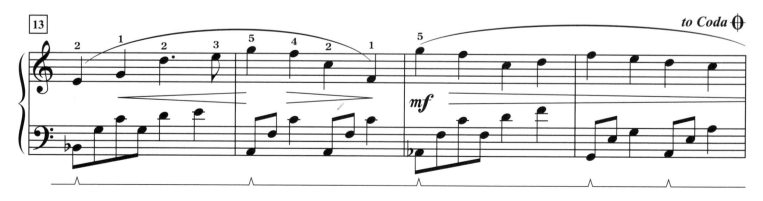

Copyright © 1995 by Alfred Music
All rights reserved..

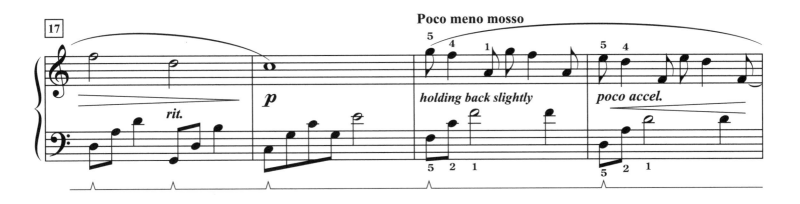

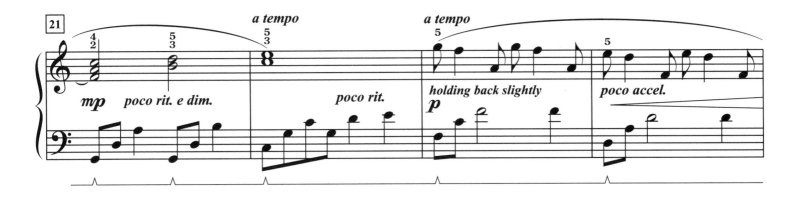

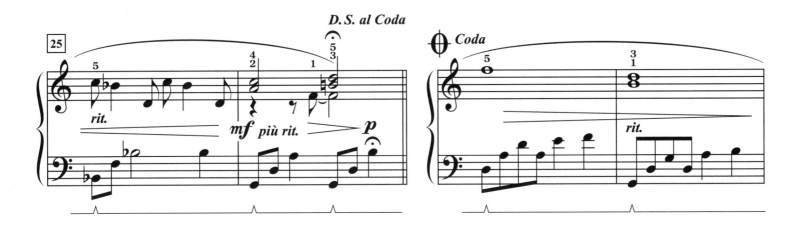

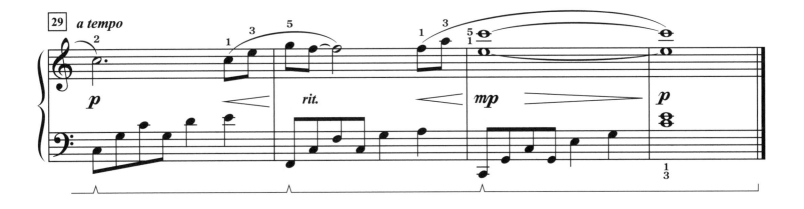

Lament

Catherine Rollin

**Slowly, but with forward motion,
expressively and with much rubato**

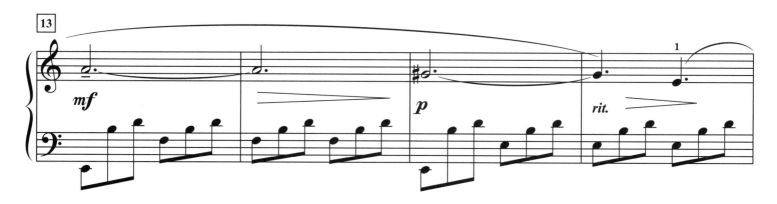

Copyright © 1995 by Alfred Music
All rights reserved..

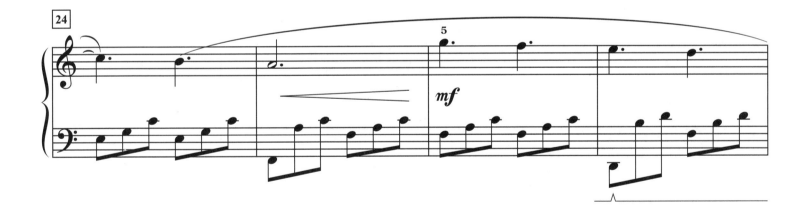

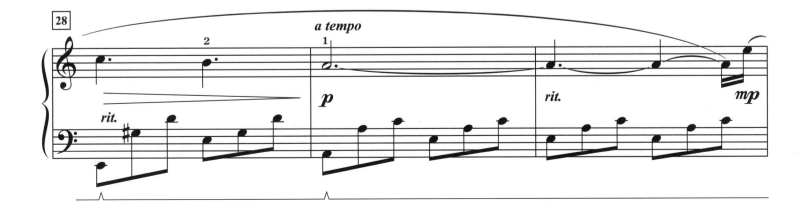

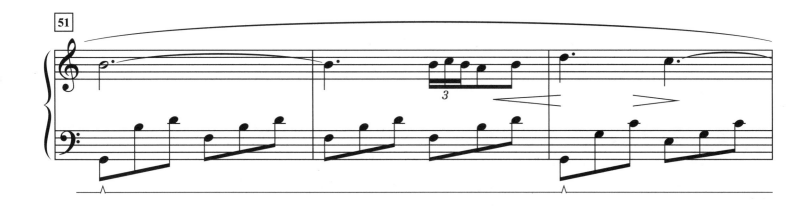

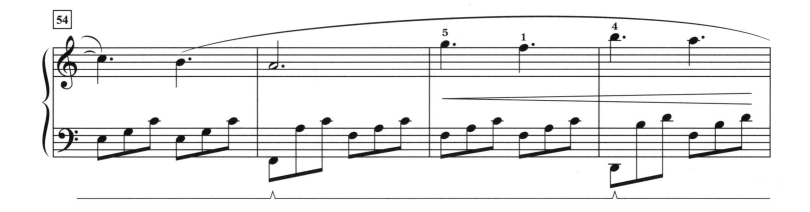

Prairie Love

Catherine Rollin

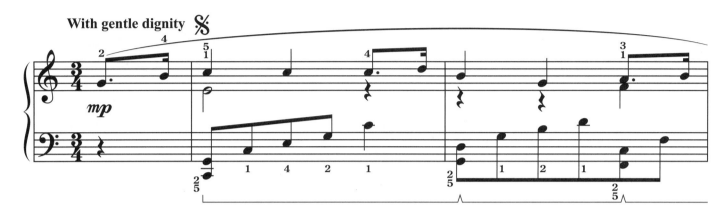

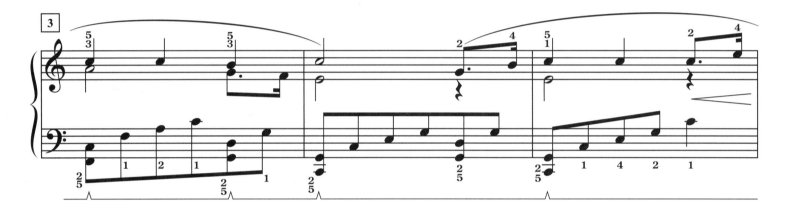

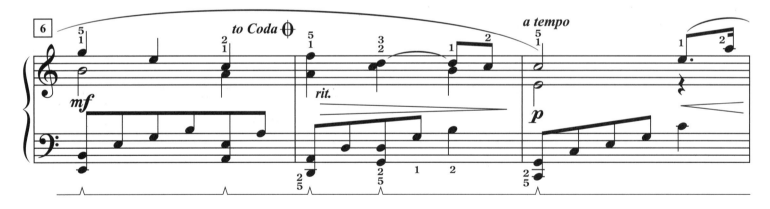

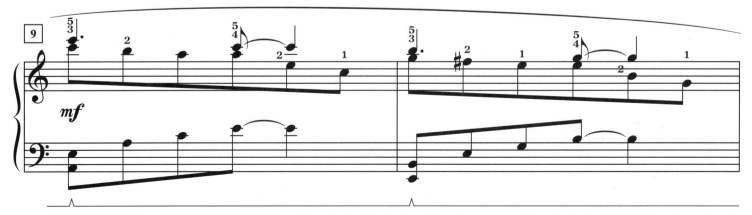

Copyright © 1995 by Alfred Music
All rights reserved..

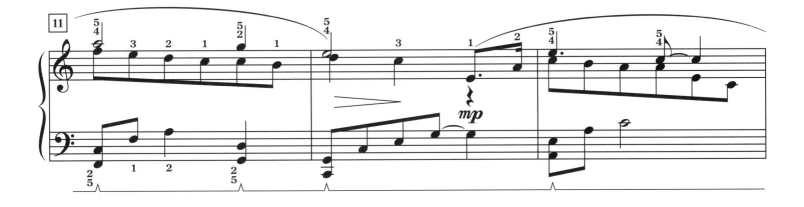

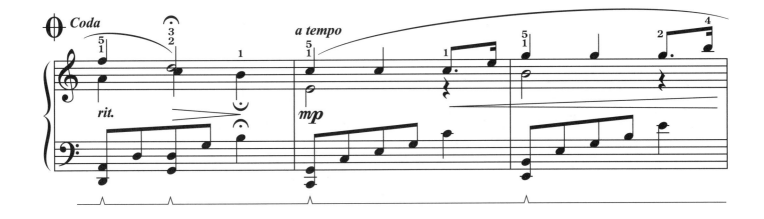

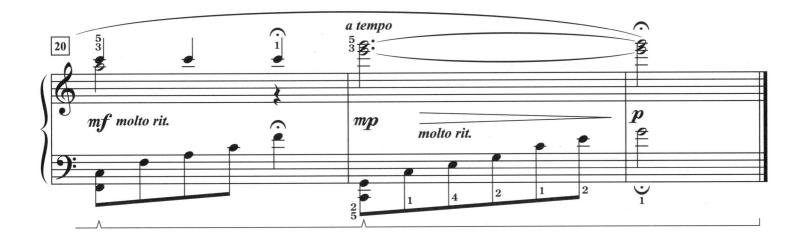

A Lovely Mood

Catherine Rollin

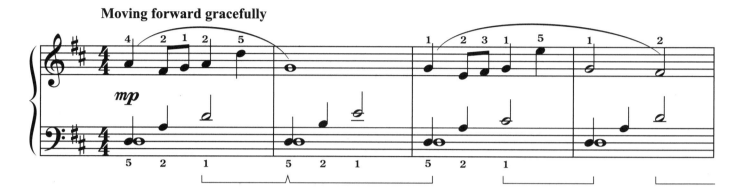

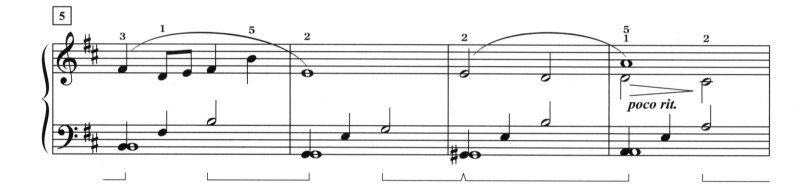

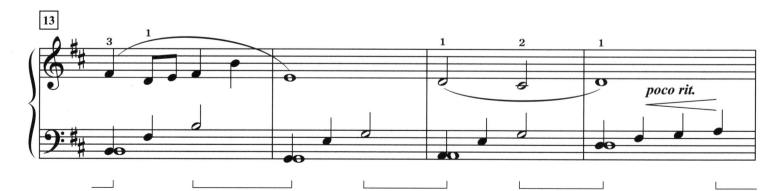

Copyright © 1995 by Alfred Music
All rights reserved..

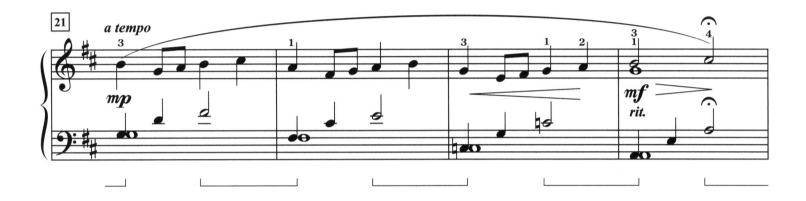

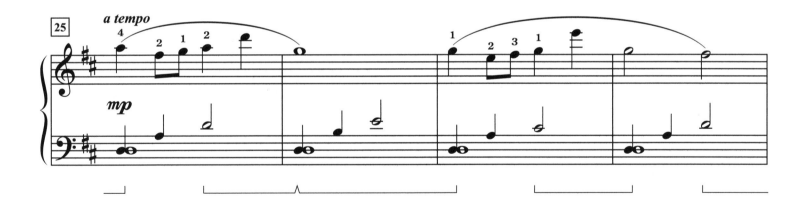

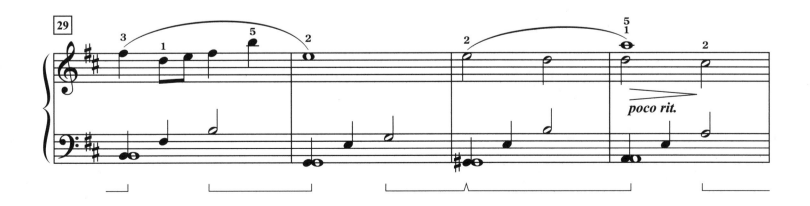

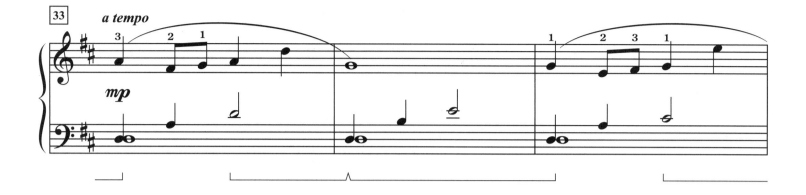

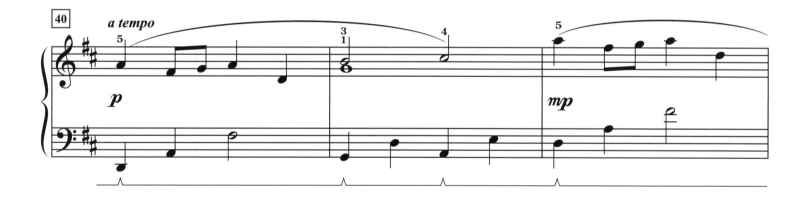

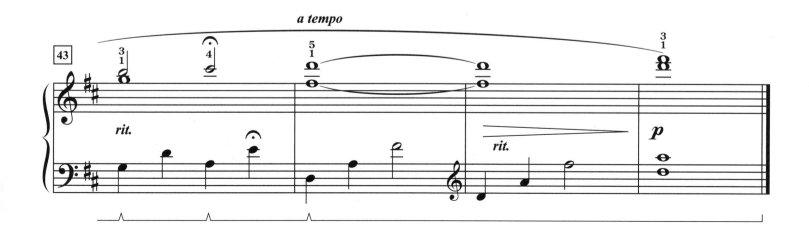

First Loss

Catherine Rollin

Slowly, but with a forward motion

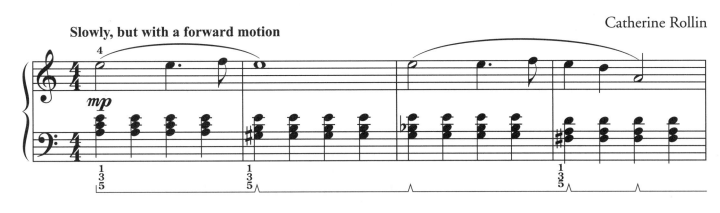

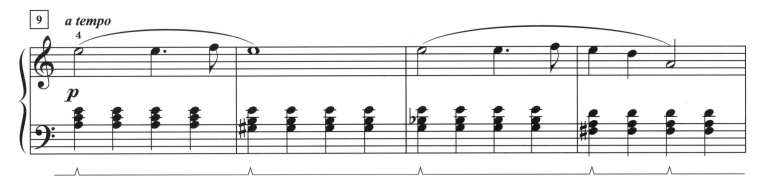

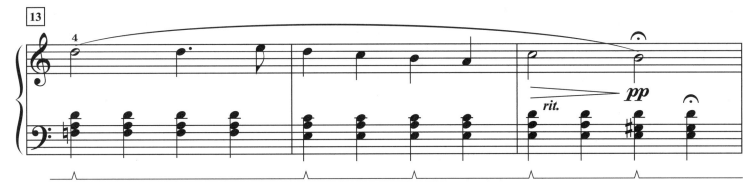

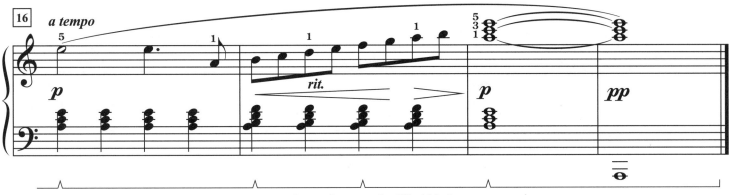

Copyright © 1995 by Alfred Music
All rights reserved..

In memory of my treasured friend
Dr. Bonnie Lynn Sherr

Sweet Elegy

Catherine Rollin

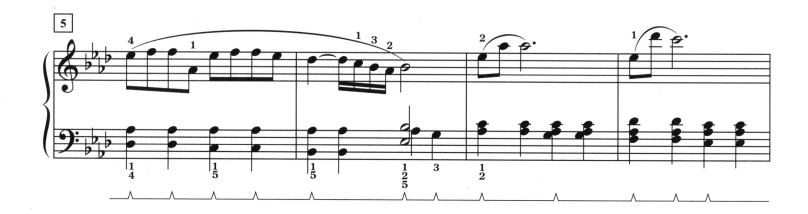

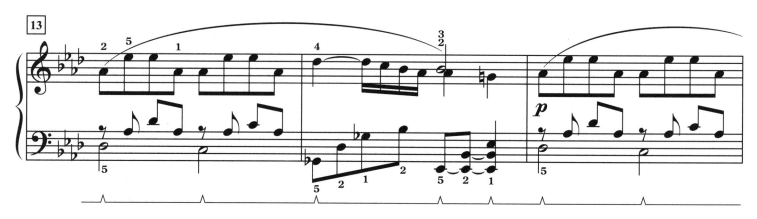

Copyright © 2010 by Alfred Music
All rights reserved..

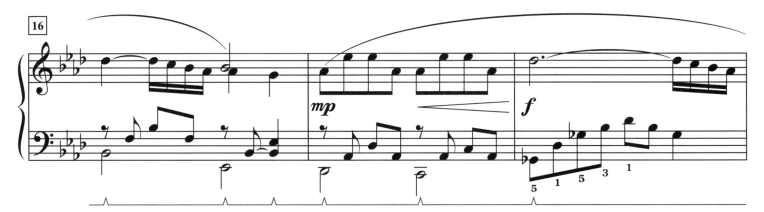

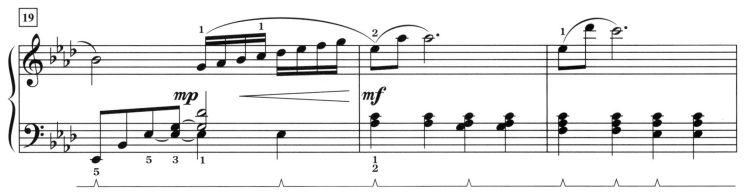

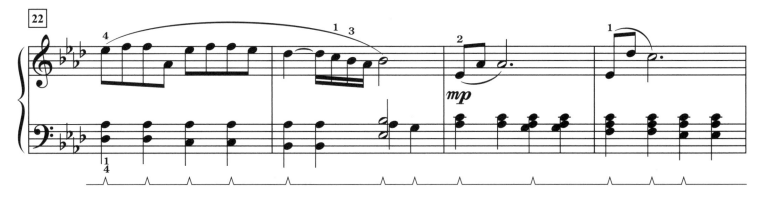

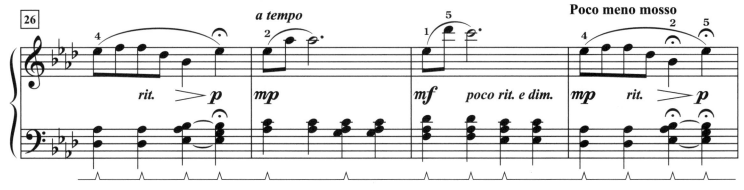

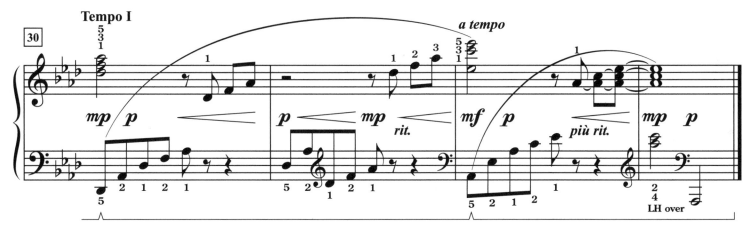

For my teacher, friend, and mentor
Dr. David Daniels

Lyric Nocturne

Catherine Rollin

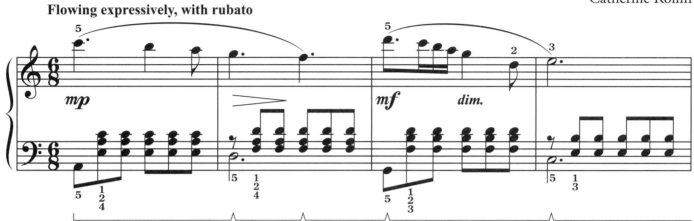

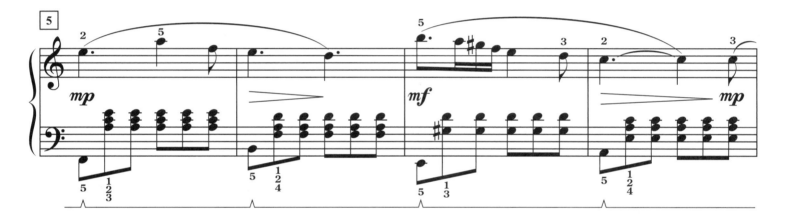

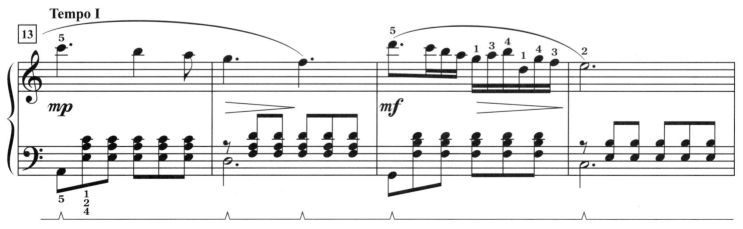

Copyright © 2010 by Alfred Music
All rights reserved..

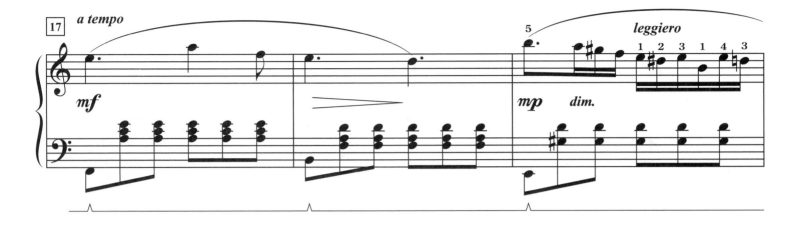

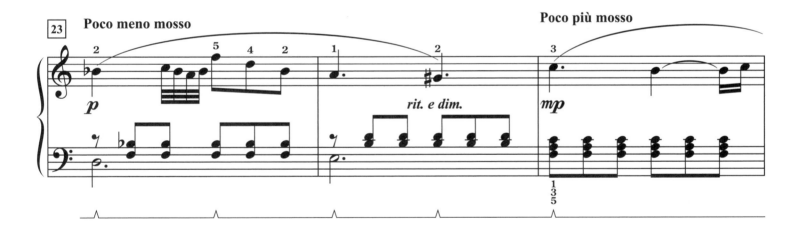

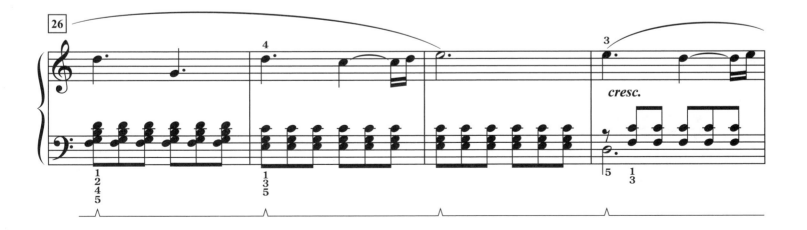

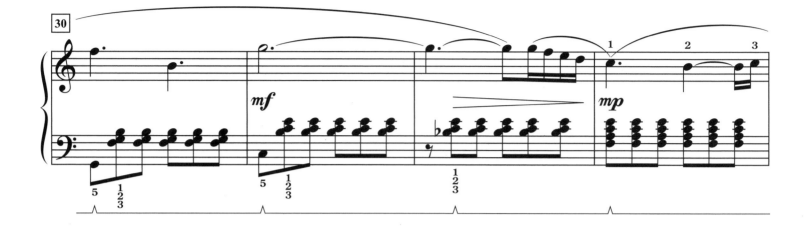

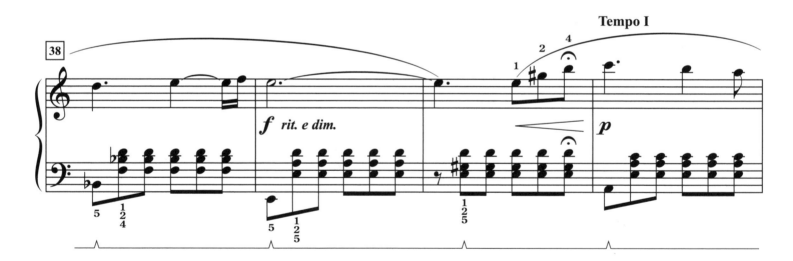

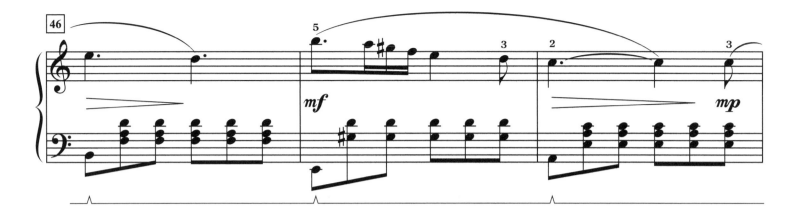

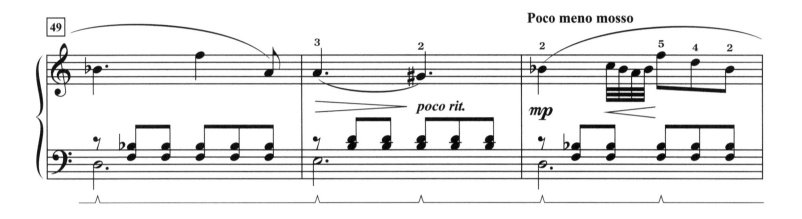

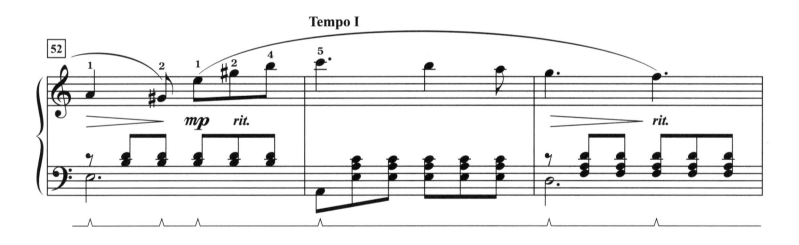

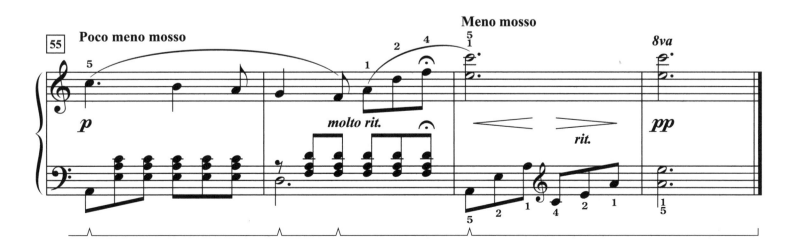

For Stephen Tu Grier

Tenderly

Catherine Rollin

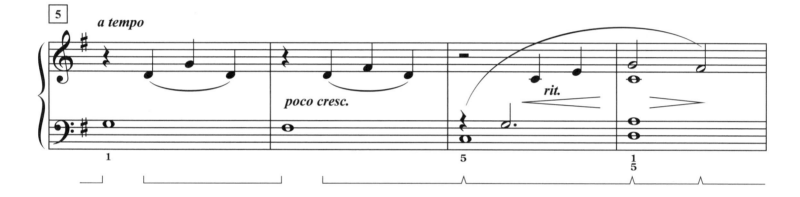

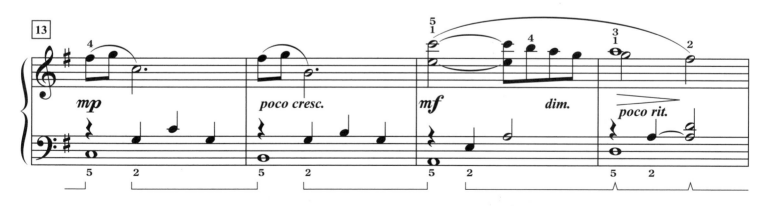

Copyright © 2010 by Alfred Music
All rights reserved..

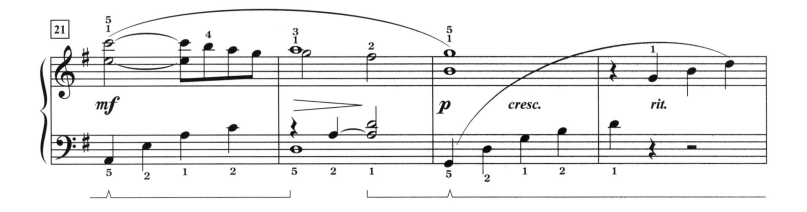

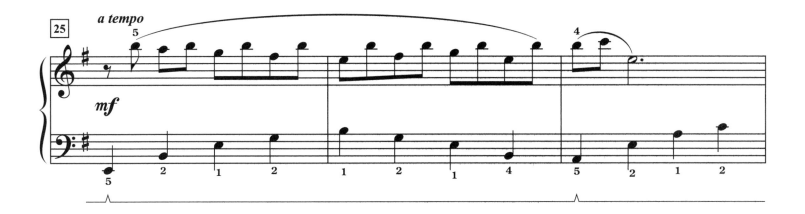

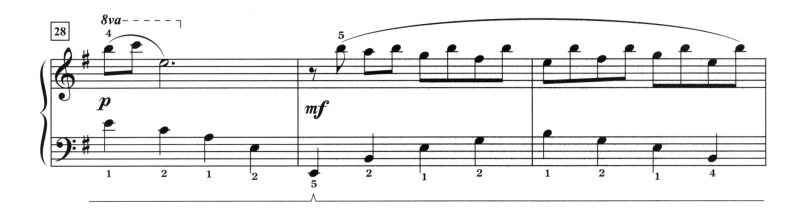

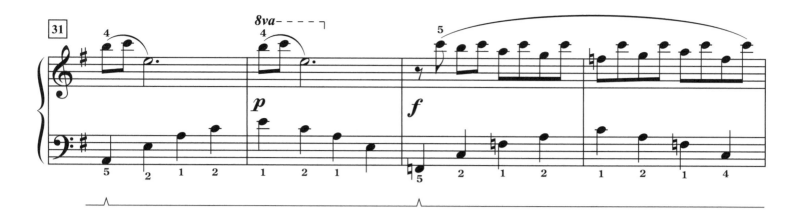

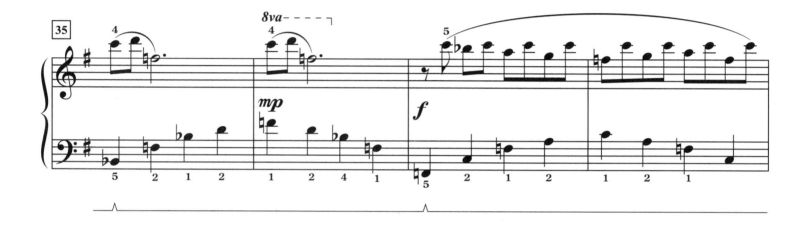

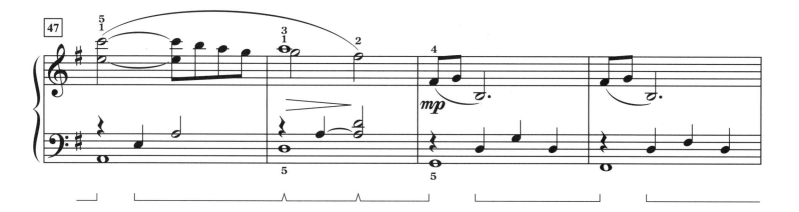

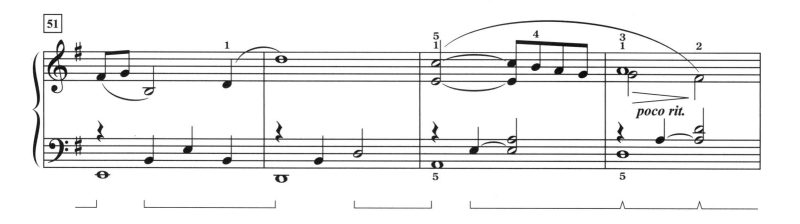

Poco meno mosso

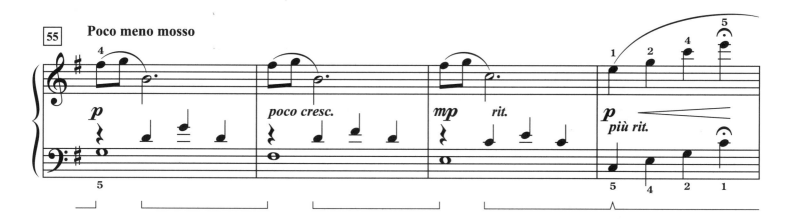

For Irwin

Pure Heart

Catherine Rollin

Flowing moderately

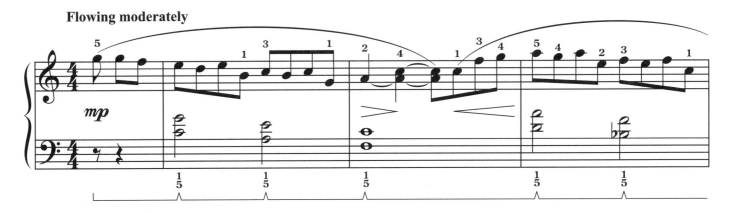

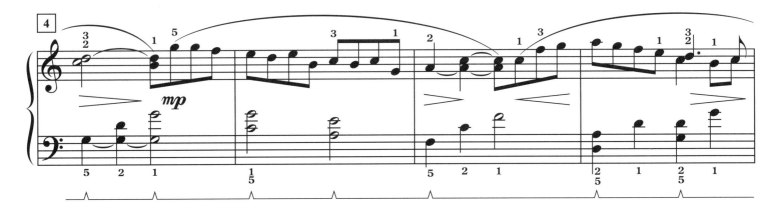

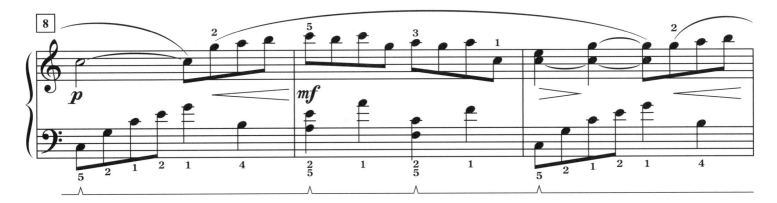

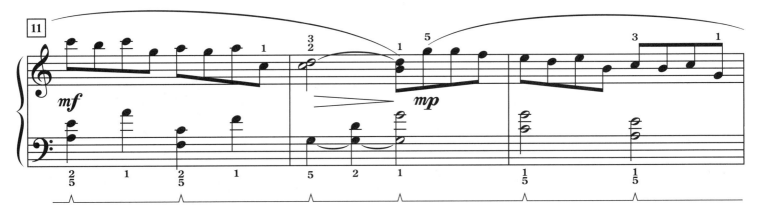

Copyright © 2010 by Alfred Music
All rights reserved..

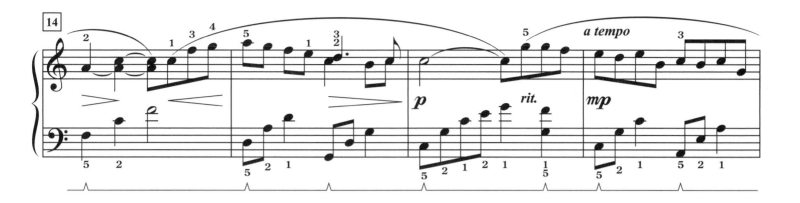

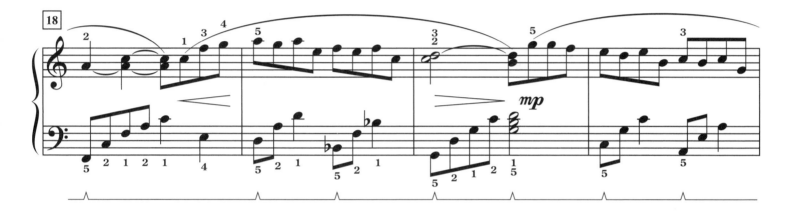

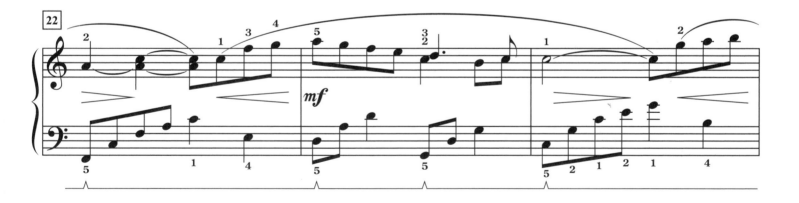

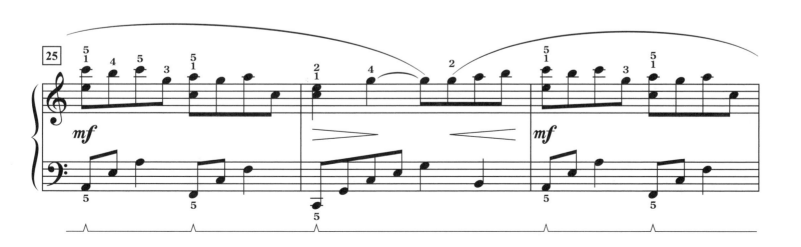

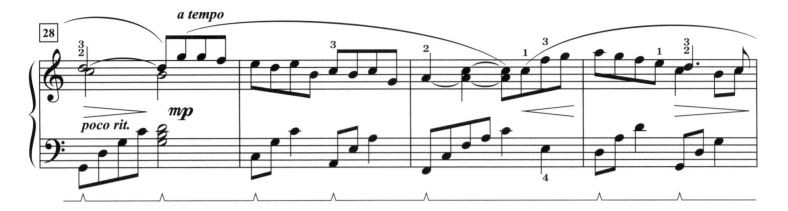

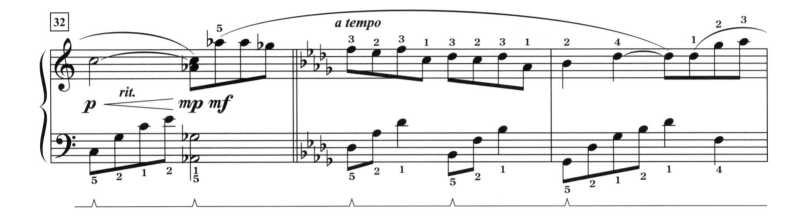

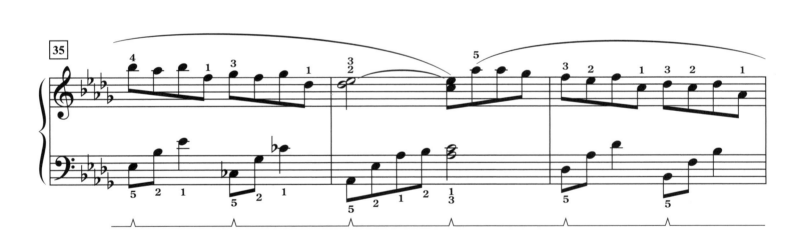

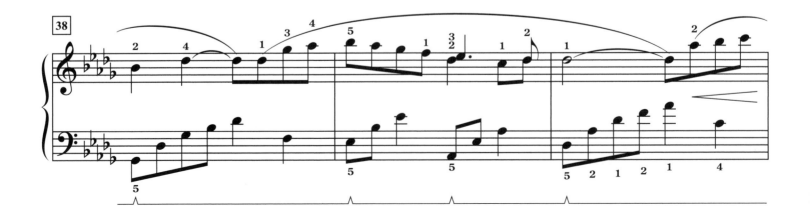

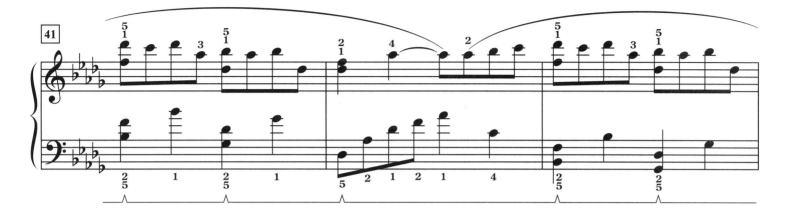

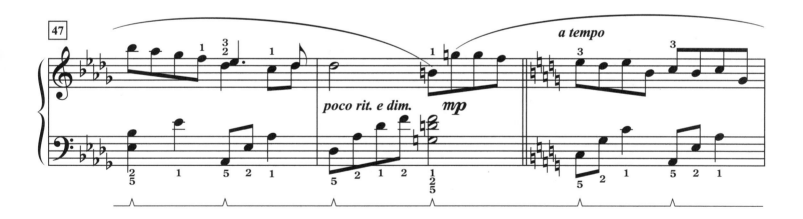

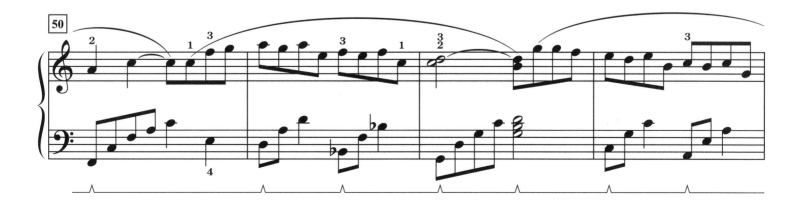

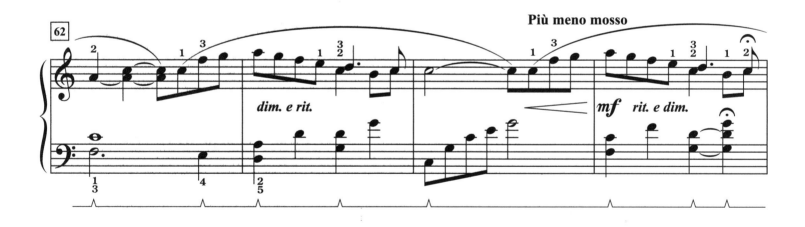

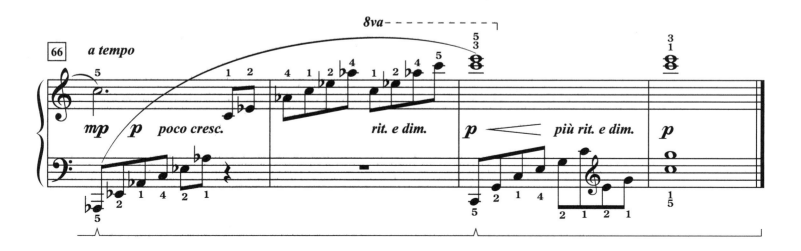

for Summer

Summer Splendor

Catherine Rollin

Flowing gently and unhurriedly

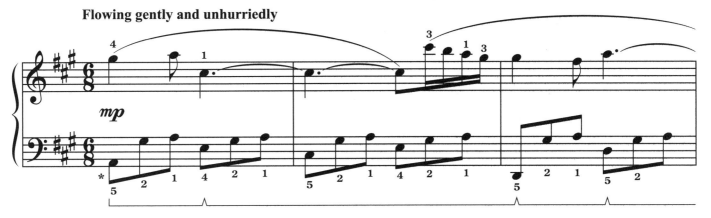

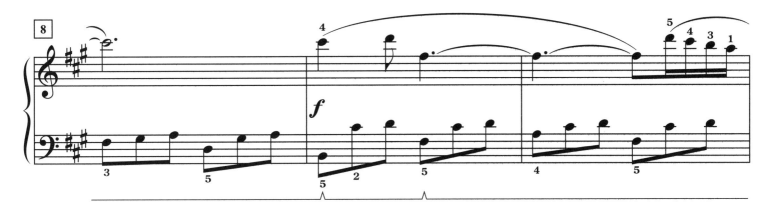

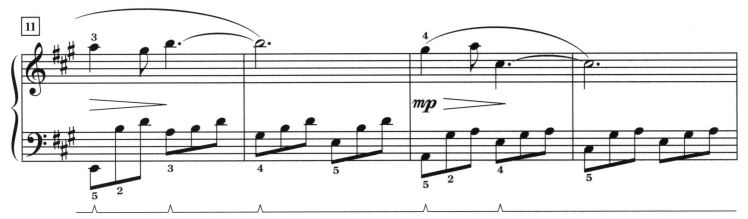

* The LH should be played very lightly to create a harmonic blend over which the RH can sing luminously.

Copyright © 2010 by Alfred Music
All rights reserved..

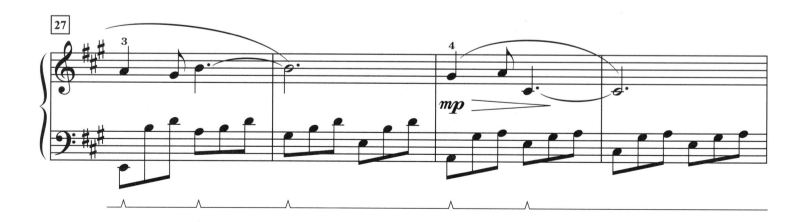

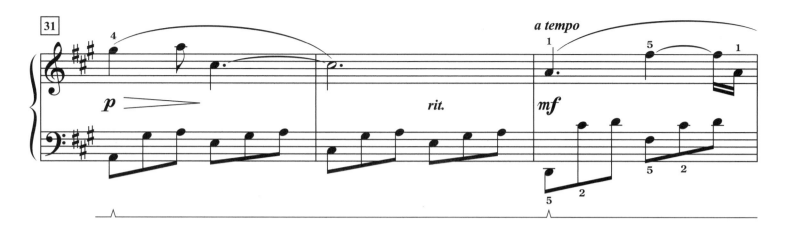

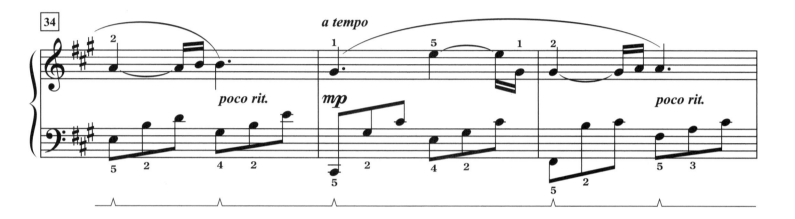

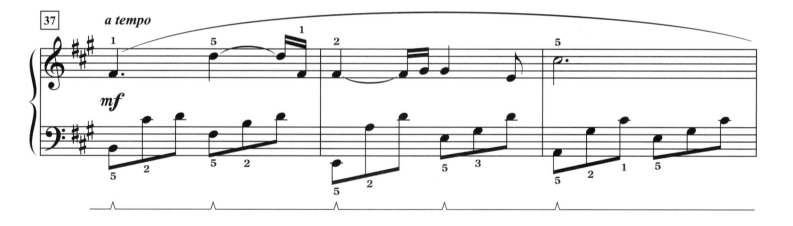

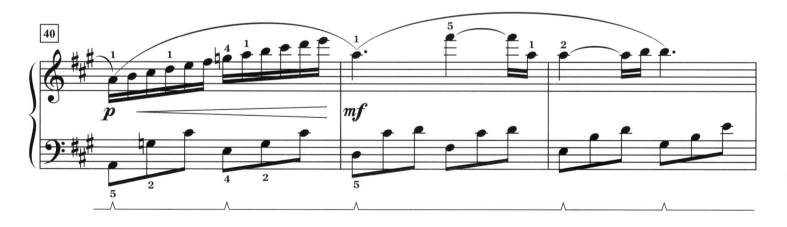

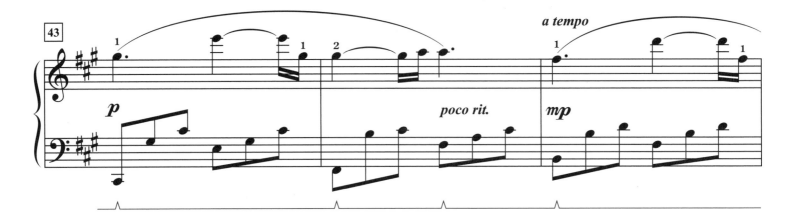

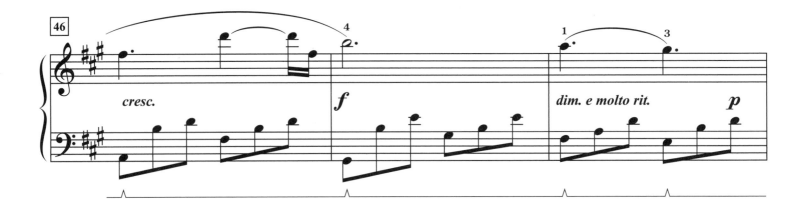

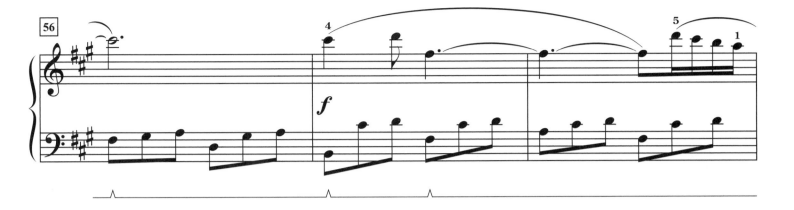

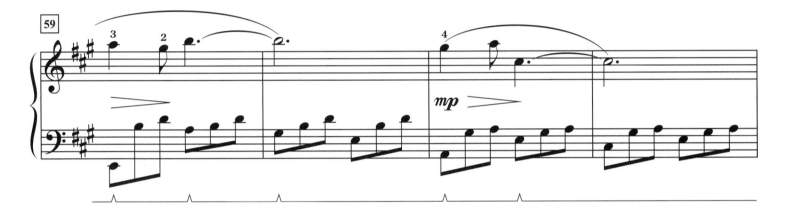

In memory of my friend Ann Ruth Kretzmer
who taught piano with love and dedication

Remembrance

Catherine Rollin

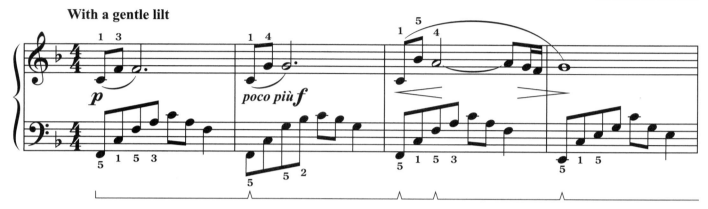

Copyright © 2010 by Alfred Music
All rights reserved..

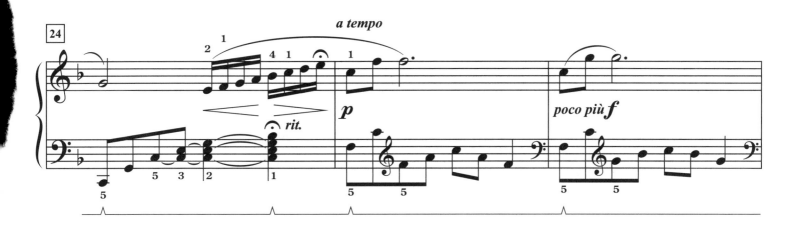

* In measures 17–18 and 21–22, the RH will be sustained by the pedal on beats 2 and 3.

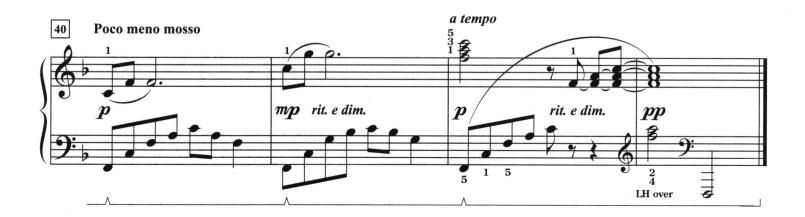